ADDICTED

From Obstacle to Opportunity

Will Richardson, M.D.

BALBOA.
PRESS
A DIVISION OF HAY HOUSE

Balboa Press books may be ordered through booksellers or by contacting:

Balboa Press
A Division of Hay House
1663 Liberty Drive
Bloomington, IN 47403
www.balboapress.com
1 (877) 407-4847

Print information available on the last page.

ISBN: 978-1-9822-1837-9 (sc)
ISBN: 978-1-9822-1839-3 (hc)
ISBN: 978-1-9822-1838-6 (e)

Library of Congress Control Number: 2018914724

Balboa Press rev. date: 2/7/2019

This book is dedicated to each and every person on the planet impacted by addiction and those who have lost the battle against addiction.

Contents

Preface

As you begin to read this book, I acknowledge you for the courage it takes to inquire into the existence of your addictions while creating access to personal growth. If you are reading this book, you are, at the very least, open to the idea that there must be an answer to everything you have survived during your human experience.

While I certainly do not represent what you will read as the ultimate truth, it may be one plausible point of view that will offer you the freedom to begin to live your life the way you've always dreamed. Until now, your life has been influenced by so many variables, and this book will only begin to address them. This is the journey you have been waiting for—an exploration of your life that will rock your world, as it has mine.

This is a summary of my own personal experience as I searched for the ultimate escape from a trap that had been laid for me before I could formulate the words for my own experiences. We were the observers, pure in form, only souls that had just chosen this existence for a purpose that became obscured by the generations before us. There were only external queues, which we could not avoid. These came in as language, shaping the circuit board of the human brain and ultimately creating an inescapable prison, denying us the freedoms we were born to enjoy. Let's begin your journey together.

Acknowledgments

I would like to acknowledge the numerous people who made this book possible. First and foremost, my mother and father, for the gift of life. My editor, Dr. Joshua M. Estrin, who was a consistent reminder that all things are possible, and to go deeper, pushing the boundaries that I had for the book.

I acknowledge my friends, who have been supportive. The jokes around publication time and the constant little chuckles they provided were relief from reality, when writing maybe was a little deep and heavy. It made me laugh to watch them walking on eggshells, at times wondering if I was observing their behaviors to recount in the book.

I acknowledge my spiritual guru who serves as a guide in life when darkness abounds, through teaching simple meditations that can heal when drugs cannot. I acknowledge my life coach, Carolina Aramburo, for always believing in me and seeing the greatness that I am even when life is falling apart. I acknowledge Werner Erhard, for his contribution to humanity as a leader in training and development. His work has altered my life forever and was an inspiration to write this book.

Introduction

The first thing I want each of you to know is that I am grateful for this opportunity to share discoveries I believe will make a difference in your life. Without you as a reader, I would not have the privilege of being an author. This book has been a long time coming, and I believe that it will provide you with clarity in life. It was transformational for me, and the work I am asking you to do is the same work I have done. I wish the same transformation for you.

First, a little bit about me as your guide on this journey. I am from an extremely small town in a rural farming community in North Carolina, and I absolutely do not consider myself a "typical doctor." I am who I am today; a product of an addict, who met a Methodist minister's daughter while she was waiting for a bus on the street, where he worked in a garage as a mechanic. The marriage was not a rose garden, to put it lightly. They later divorced, and my mother raised four kids on welfare, with the help of others in the community, both church and local.

I saw addiction destroy my father's life and remove him from his children, whom he loved so very much. I vowed that my life would not be centered on addiction. I had not a clue how inescapable that sentence would be. Addiction would be the theme of my life, resulting in many learning experiences and growth nodes, as I am not one who believes in "mistakes" or "problems." These words are the language of addiction. Addiction took my father's life, and it is my soul's purpose to ensure that it doesn't take another's, including my own.

While I am a board certified medical doctor, I want you to know that I am a human with a body of experiences not dissimilar from your own. If our work together is going to make a difference, allow me the grace to be a person and not a profession. Many of you may have an opinion of physicians that influences how you view and listen to us. We are at a point in humanity where our evolution is being driven by external rather than internal forces. *I do not claim anything that you will read to be the "truth," the "only way," or the "solution."*

This collection of words you are reading is only one possible view of the human experience, laid out by a kid, me. I grew up in a single-wide trailer, raised by a Christian mother on welfare, and I later worked at restaurants and held three jobs to get through college. I then went on to go to college even though I dropped out of high school in the tenth grade for being bullied and labeled as "the faggot." I considered suicide at one point to escape it all, but I honored my mother so much, and I knew this would create a world of suffering I did not want to leave her with. After graduating from a small state college summa cum laude, I went on to get into medical school, even though everyone told me that I would never make it in. I did make it. The odds were completely stacked against me for my next dream, that of becoming a dermatologist, which at the time was the most desirable competitive specialty in medicine. Yet, I accomplished that too.

As a board-certified dermatologist, I took a position in Florida, where my father had lived and died. I was fired from my first job and left abandoned to fend for myself in an already saturated community of skincare providers. Knowing absolutely nothing about business, I literally used a booklet called "How to Start a Dermatology Practice," provided by the American Academy of Dermatology, and checked off the boxes, launching a successful medical practice that has cared for more than 18,000 people to date.

During this time as a business owner, I allowed myself to experience everything. I delved into the "rooms" to gain a greater understanding of what my father experienced while alive and also to gain personal control over my own addictive nature. The next stop was a variety of training and development courses. I went on to lead seminars using methodologies created and inspired by Werner Erhard.

I visited spiritual places from my youth and Christian background, including the Holy Lands and countless churches. I explored Buddhism and visited many *wats* (temples). Always looking for answers, I spent a week with a spiritual guru, Sai Maa, convinced that she could offer me all the answers, but this was not the case. I needed to dig more deeply into the works of personal development leaders such as Eckhart Tolle and Gary Zukav. I came to realize that all these experiences could be synthesized into this book. This is not to discount, dishonor, or diminish the extraordinary impact all these various leaders and guides have had on the life I live today, as this book would not exist without every single moment and thousands of hours of personal development.

So, while perhaps you thought you should be listening to a physician, my simple request remains: allow me to lead you through this inquiry as a *human*. Allow me the grace to let your judgments fall away, and allow me to be without a label, whether gay, straight, black, white, Christian, Buddhist, physician, or teacher. No matter who you are and where you are in your process, you are ready for this transformation. You deserve it! This book will make a difference for you, no matter what continent you are on. This is an audacious claim and one I am committed to fulfilling. I have done all the work that I ask of you in this book. Though it's not easy at times, it's worth every moment, so let's get started!

How This Book Works

For many of you, you probably just thought this was going to be a good read that you plow through, taking away insights as you go. It is perfectly fine to do that. You can certainly find value this way if you choose to do so. Another way to engage with this book is to see it as it was designed, as a tool to guide you where to look into your life and what to look for, very much like a scavenger hunt map, with much the same excitement. We will be looking at your life, with you as the *active observer*. This book also includes inquiries that are designed to allow you to remain active in your observations. You may consider reading it with a friend and completing the inquiries together.

What are "inquiries"? Inquiries are opportunities to step outside your everyday life and create awareness of yourself by examining a specific aspect of your life. Throughout the book, there may be moments where you may experience emotions, or recall things that you didn't want to deal with, or things you didn't know about yourself. When those moments arise, simply take three deep breaths and allow the emotions to pass. Once they have passed, return to the book.

Liberation: A Human Experiment

Wherever you are right now, take a look at your surroundings. Look at the person sitting next to you, look at the room you are in, notice the sounds that you hear easily, and then notice the background sounds. Simply notice your environment. With over seven billion people on this planet, this is where you ended up being with all of your current accomplishments, successes, failures, and disappointments. This is how it went for you so far. Experience the emotions to their fullest, and do not hold back.

For some of you, this may cause feelings of excitement, joy, and fulfillment. For others, it may elicit sadness, disappointment, hopelessness, and resignation that things will always be this way. You have worked very hard to get where you are at this moment, and more often than not, it wasn't easy. There were some struggles along the way and moments when you had to expand what you saw as possible for you to accomplish to get here.

You are a human being on a journey, and the story will end the same for us all. You are born, grow old, and die. It's really that simple and could be the summary of your entire existence. So much happens between birth and death, and you just observed a glimpse of your individuality and uniqueness. At the same time, begin to open yourself to talking about your experiences.

As you read this book, you will begin to find that we are all very similar. Your life could be described as blinded imprisonment with a life sentence of hopeful existence, and missing the mark tainted with partial moments of fulfillment. This may seem upsetting or alarming. It is not the truth. It is the position that, if you take it, will have this book make a difference for you.

In reading this book, there is a promise that will be delivered: Liberation will happen. The significance you place on areas of life may shift, and that's okay. It is time for us to evolve rapidly to make the difference for future inhabitants. What this particular evolution will take is letting go of the significance we have spent creating around us to ensure our personal happiness.

The invitation is to write down what comes to mind every time you have a reaction to things you read in this book. This list, short or long, will be of use and make a difference at the end in liberating you from your personal prison. This imprisonment is not visible, but it impacts you as if it were a physical structure. Your imprisonment is created by silent addictions that have been growing indolently, like a hidden virus inside your mind. The walls of your captivity are an energy field reinforced by addiction and focused on diminishing your life experiences. Let's start to explore the life imprisonment of humanity in the context that every one of us are addicts in disguise.

Addiction: The Inescapable Destiny

Human beings are addicts. Addiction has been a part of us since the moment we attempted to walk. There was such profound risk in that moment, and we failed time and time again. Then, suddenly, we got it right, and the phenomenon called walking followed. The experience of getting it right was extraordinarily exquisite for us in and of itself, but walking gave us an experience of something we couldn't put into words: independence.

This was the first reward we accomplished on our own as human beings. You see, every other reward prior to this moment was given to us. "No," you may have just said as you read that. Consider that all you had to do was cry, and you received whatever you needed or wanted shall I say, automatically—food, water, milk, and perhaps the intoxicating reward of attention. It was absolutely the easiest living; all you had to do was cry, and the world organized itself around you for your survival and satisfaction.

Walking, however, required some assistance initially. But the moment you completed the action solo, you became a new human being. You were unconquerable in your own eyes, and that carried you through the environment where things were significantly larger than you, and you navigated with the courage of a samurai warrior. Every new room, person, situation, and place was inviting. You even had your own cheerleading team, as others around you cheered you on and celebrated this heroic event.

After learning to walk, you were able to take the things you previously had to cry for. There was a twist to this time in your life in that, yes, you could simply now go and get the things you wanted. But you very quickly learned that limitations came with independence and freedom. Suddenly, something very drastic happened: discipline.

Guess what you did when you were first told no. That's right, you went right back to crying. But this time it didn't work, no matter how loudly you cried. What did you possibly do next? You fell to the ground because you knew before you could walk that lying on the ground plus crying equaled reward. That failed you too, by the way. *Where did I ever go wrong?* you wondered in your very rudimentary language. No matter the logic you came up with or the methods you tried to receive the reward, the only answer was to succumb and be controlled. This worked for a while for you for very long time, taking you into your teen years.

During your teen years, there was one theme: "resist being controlled." Of course, part of that time was self-discovery through a number of vehicles, always with an underlying resistance to be controlled. If you take a walk through an average day in your life, you were taught to brush your teeth, dress, go to school at a certain time, and sit in a class for a certain amount of time, controlled by a bell. When the bell rang, a certain behavior called "changing classes" occurred, and you began to experience a phenomenon called "longing." Remember how you waited for that bell to ring? Minutes seemed like hours, and during that period of longing, there was nothing really wrong, but you couldn't wait for that bell to ring. Why? It signified the arrival of a moment of freedom. At least until the next period of control began. School perhaps was less about giving you knowledge than preparing you for society, where control is a key experience.

Ultimately, the school day ended, and you could return home, where you experienced more control. There was homework that had to be done. For some, chores had to be completed. Then maybe you got a little taste of freedom and could choose what you would like to do with friends in the community. But only until it was time to go to bed, where you slept the number of hours determined to be sufficient to make you a healthy human being. And then you started all over again. At this point, you may begin to get a glimpse of how exhausting this is.

These periods of freedom were the beginning of your brain creating pleasure at an experiential level, as opposed to a reflexive, primitive phenomenon. What brought an experience of pleasure in the brain began to shape your choices and fuel the ever-growing, never-ending resistance to control.

At the same time, another phenomenon was occurring. An addiction to pleasure was being fueled, running completely in the background. It's the old adage, "Hindsight is 20/20." It's easy to look back and distinguish this now, but is it something one can really take as the case? Yes. We can allow it to be a useful bit of information, shaping a future that will be a form of delayed gratification as opposed to immediate reward.

What difference does it make even to have this conversation and write this book for you to read? Things are absolutely okay, and life will happen. You will get to live the life you choose. It's easy to have a conversation about things that don't work, but what does it take to actually implement them in your daily life? That is where breaking the cycle of addiction is the greatest step in our evolution, allowing future generations to enjoy this extraordinary planet we call home. It requires you to confront everything in life you think is normal and consider a new way of living. It's not forgetting everything you know. It's not taking on a new religion, eating new food, giving away your riches, or releasing anything you identify as uniquely you. How to escape can only be answered by first looking at the addictions on this planet that do not discriminate against race, religion, culture, or socioeconomic class. This book is for every human being on the planet, not for one person. Let's continue the journey now, putting aside our judgments, and explore this with an open mind.

What immediately arises for you as a thought when you hear the word "addiction" is not the truth. It is simply a construct created against a background of morality and virtues powerfully influenced by experiences. We see the person on the street begging for money or food, and immediately we think, *It's probably for drugs*. Perhaps you would even think, *If people didn't spend all their money on drugs, they would have money for food*. Do you see the lack of compassion and abundance of judgment?

What if we were to accept Adam, in the story of creation, as the first beggar? There are ascribed underlying motives, however. If you remove the story and observe the action in real time without a narrative, it was simply one human being offering to nurture another human being in that moment. For centuries, the story has been a powerful influence. Perhaps this is where our first notions of "good" and "bad" arose in our life experiences. Why would anyone see the action of offering fruit to another human being as anything other than an act of compassion?

Let's get very real. What is meant by the word "addiction"?

Addiction: "The state of being enslaved to a habit or practice or to something that is psychologically or physically habit-forming, as narcotics, to such an extent that cessation causes severe trauma." [1] Historically, "c. 1600, 'tendency' of habits, pursuits, etc.; 1640s as state of being self-addicted, from Latin *addictionem* (nominative *addictio*) an awarding, a devoting, noun of action from past participle stem of *addicere* (see addict). Earliest sense was less severe: "inclination,

---

[1] Dictionary.com. http://www.dictionary.com/browse/addiction?s=t.

penchant," but this has become obsolete. In main modern sense, it is first attested 1906, in reference to opium (there is an isolated instance from 1779 concerning tobacco)[2].

First of all, it seems quite apparent that we as human beings have manipulated language to fit our world. The word was historically (i.e., at the turn of the seventeenth century) associated with the "state of being self-addicted" and later became associated with medical substances. Was it that we changed our focus from addiction as the fulfillment of self-needs to using it as a tool to judge others, intentional or coincidence, such that we deflected the attention from ourselves to a substance? Or was it a subconscious mechanistic action that would allow for the disease to be present undistinguished within human beings? I offer that this was a well-thought, intended action, the source of which we will never know.

Your perspective of addiction may be already evolving, and you may be seeing yourself a bit of an addict. It is perfectly okay and a part of the journey and process of the book. As I mentioned earlier, simply allow yourself moments, where needed, to take a break, close the book, reflect, and then return to complete the work.

Are you rewarding yourself with money, sex, shopping, eating, or creating the perfect post on social media that will foster hundreds to thousands of "likes"? Perhaps your reward is acknowledgment or admiration. Begin to see the drugs that you consume daily. You may be experiencing a bit of anxiety, fear, or an urge to walk away from this book, and that would be simply more of the addiction winning the game. How? You would get to continue on the course you are on without any evolution in the realm of addiction.

Lastly, notice the use of the word "enslavement." If you don't believe you are enslaved by your set of actions that result in delivery

---

[2] Online Etymology Dictionary. https://www.etymonline.com/word/addiction.

of the reward, then go ahead and interrupt that action and delay or remove the reward entirely. Set down your phone. Turn it on silent. Feel the pull to pick it up again. Skip your normal mealtime and notice the urge to eat. Even more so, notice that you may not even be hungry.

When we think about addiction, we often blame the addict. We may even think for a moment about the addict and how terrible it is for people to actually be addicted to anything. "These people should be put away." "They should be punished." "They are a disgrace to society." I feel this point of view is shared by most human beings and that it has been a barrier to moving forward and actually treating the disease. Eckhart Tolle stresses throughout his teachings that awareness creates an opportunity for something unique to arise. However, as long as we are not aware of what is currently there, there is no need to change the condition. *If the condition is not distinguished, it cannot be treated.*

However, once the condition actually has been diagnosed, then there is real opportunity for healing to occur. I propose that is where we are now concerning our human addiction. For too long, we have been unable to treat what lies at the heart of the human condition simply because we've been unwilling to see ourselves as a part of the problem. It's a problem that is plaguing our lives and our experiences on this planet. We are now taking a step together in this book, and taking the position for ourselves, that we all are affected by addiction. There is evidence to show that you're an addict if you're willing to look around and attempt to interrupt your daily routine, attempt to interrupt your ritualistic patterns of behavior, attempt to interrupt your point of view. Allow yourself to become so present to all the addictions you have in your life that judgment falls away. Allow yourself to be become disgusted with your own condition in your own life.

See how your addiction is influencing the way in which you raise your children. See how your own addiction is being woven into the fabric of their "genetics," from which they will teach future generations, never addressing the underlying condition, which is that, as human beings, we no longer know how to create. We are a stimulus-and-response phenomenon. We spend our entire lives reacting to perceived threats. When did this begin? How do we stop it? The interruption is simply to take the case that your whole life has been controlled by addiction, and it's been going on completely unnoticed in your blind spot.

What is the blind spot? A blind spot is that which you cannot see in yourself that has brought stagnation to your life for decades. When it is revealed, the result is liberation. The time is now. Our very existence as a species depends on breaking this addiction. Addiction to what, you may ask? Our current conditions of living, for one. We must have oil, even though it disrupts our planet. We must have power to fuel our homes, even though the source from which it comes is poisoning our rivers and our environment. We must have tobacco crops that are dried and sold as smoking tobacco or chewing tobacco, both of which cause cancer. We must have access to cars, which comes at the cost of fossil fuels. What are some of the "must-haves" in your life that you're unwilling to live without?

Complete Inquiry 1, then return to continue.

There is an energy field being created within the conversation that this book brings into existence. Inside energy fields, things become possible that once were not. Inside an energy field, particles begin to move and synchronize with time. The absolute greatest outcome of this book would be to share what you discover about yourself through this work so that others can begin to have the same types of self-discoveries and transformational experiences that you can now access. After participating in this conversation, realms of life will evolve. There will be actions that you will not recognize. At first, these may shake your own existence. It may startle you, and you may question what has happened. Don't worry. There will be moments when the addiction will prevail, but if there are moments for yourself in which you become fluid in thought, allowing for newly created spaces to arise, then you will have fulfilled the intention of this book.

Pleasure

One of the first things we have to deal with is how lazy we have become. One of the things this book is not is just a simple read. This book is designed to have you go to war with and work on life. Not you, not your problems, but life. You may be pleasantly surprised to discover some of your problems disappearing, but don't worry; new ones will arise, or you may find yourself creating new ones that are bigger than ever. You may even come to embrace and love having problems in your life.

It is incredible how much we human beings love the experience of pleasure. It's the purpose of your entire life. You may or may not be aware of it, but it's there in the background. It shapes your actions, the way you listen, what you smell over other smells, what you taste over other tastes. Ultimately, it creates your whole world around you right now. I will share my own example in my life. As you listen to each example I share with you throughout the book, I want you to practice listening in a certain way: listen while at the same time looking into your life and seeing how it would fit for you in whatever you are dealing with currently. I know this may be new for some of you, and for some of you it may be familiar. Here we go.

I enjoy financial independence and security. It truly brings me pleasure beyond belief at the end of the day. I will go to any length and sacrifice and do whatever it takes to make sure that I am financially independent and secure. In real life, what this requires is for me to work in my office, pulling the load of two physicians each day to enjoy a nice house with a beautiful backyard and a luxury yacht in the water to enjoy on the weekends.

Now, remember, your example of what brings pleasure may not be the same as mine, and notice how you began to compare, and maybe even judge, as you read what I just shared with you. That's just more of the addict in you, so let that just be for now.

Human beings are driven by pleasure, and you can find sufficient evidence of this just by turning on the television or by watching your "regular" shows. Looking for yourself, what is it that brings you the experience of true pleasure? Let's explore the definition so that we are clear on what we are experiencing and referencing.

> Pleasure: "The state or feeling of being pleased; enjoyment or satisfaction derived from what is to one's liking; gratification; delight."

When you take a look at what actually happens in the brain, there is simply a release of a variety of chemicals, resulting in a specific feeling, mediated mainly by dopamine, in a small mass of tissue located at the base of the brain, called the *nucleus accumbens*. This region responds to a variety of signals common to most humans (e.g., food, sex, drugs, massage). On the other hand, this same region of the brain can be stimulated in certain individuals by perceiving they are "doing the work of God" by flying a plane into a building or pulling out an automatic rifle in a school and opening fire. Perhaps now you are a little more interested in this small mass of tissue.

This region of the brain has been referred to as being a part of the "lizard brain."

"Well, I am way more advanced than a lizard," you may say to yourself. You may possibly feel an immediate sense of insult, an increase in your pulse, sweating, anger, and the urge to throw this book. Guess what? That is your limbic system, your "lizard brain," at work. It governs the "six Fs," as we will call them here: "fight, flight, fear, feeding, freezing up, and fornication."[3]

Now, this lizard brain isn't exactly useless, as you will see. Certainly, if the space around you were to begin to tremble right now, suggestive of an earthquake, you wouldn't want the brain to take several minutes to process and think out the following scenario verbatim:

"Something unusual just happened. I think I should feel afraid. I need to move my eyes to look around and assess what is happening. I have to find a memory for what it is called when the earth shakes violently below me without reason. Perhaps, next I should extend the arms to balance and then coordinate the feet for stability. I notice the walls are crumbling; therefore, I have to increase blood pressure and heart rate to allow sufficient blood flow to the muscles, which I will now engage to run, while finding an opening in the wall that is called a door, and then I will aim perfectly so that I can pass through the door with velocity to avoid hitting the sides."

No. This is all completely automatic. There is no thought to this process, thankfully.

Similarly, there is no thought process to eating. For human beings who are starving, in the absence of moral or religious conviction,

[3] Troncale, Joseph, M.D. "Your Lizard Brain." Psychology Today. April 22, 2014. https://www.psychologytoday.com/us/blog/where-addiction-meets-your-brain/201404/your-lizard-brain.

when you put food in front of them, they simply begin to perform the act of eating. There is no similar thought process of figuring out how to eat. You don't have to think about how to chew and how to swallow. Now, this may sound silly, and you may think, "Well, I was taught to chew." Perhaps you were not, or you did not need to see chewing to be able to know what to do with your teeth. You may think to yourself, "No, I was taught to eat by my parents. There are cute videos of this." Were you really learning to eat, or were they simply fulfilling a memory of what they were taught? What was really taking place was more of the natural activity of the reptilian brain—nurturing. The argument to this point is that dogs and other mammals are not taught to chew. Food is placed in front of them and they simply feed. They are simply eating to survive and sustain life.

Aside from these essential functions, this portion of the human brain is also what has you wake up in the morning and never think twice about how you are going to get from your bed and into your car to get to work. Think for a moment and ask yourself, *What was the car make and model that was in front of me on the way to work?* You weren't even aware of that.

Furthermore, there was no thought process involved while you miraculously sent a text, checked your social media, and still managed to arrive safely at your destination. Even though there are now laws against doing such activities while driving, you still did this. More about this will come in later chapters. For now, just begin to notice the automaticity that is an overwhelming part of your life.

As human beings evolved, we developed higher order processes and tapped into how to stimulate this "reward system" in our brain. What is a reward? Wikipedia provides us a quick definition:

> Reward is the attractive and motivational property of a stimulus that induces appetitive behavior, also

known as approach behavior, and consummatory behavior. In its description of a rewarding stimulus (i.e., 'a reward'), a review on reward neuroscience noted, "any stimulus, object, event, activity, or situation that has the potential to make us approach and consume it is by definition a reward.[4]

Operant behavior gives a good definition for rewards. Anything that makes an individual come back for more is a positive reinforcer and therefore a reward. [5]

We sacrifice so much in our lives, impacting the quality of our lives, to experience the reward providing pleasure—all for the fulfillment of addiction. The impact is never where we immediately think which is within ourselves. The extent of the impact is never fully appreciated, and often we attribute it to the addiction alone. In the end, there is only the substance, situation, or thing that is the object of desire in the outside world. All the ways in which we react are in the end by our own choosing. We say things like, "The devil made me do it" or "That was just the drugs talking." In the end, there is no responsibility or control in that mentality. Of course, that does leave an opening to revisit the situation, substance, or thing that is the object of desire again.

This is an excellent opportunity for an assignment, and I will preface yours with sharing a little about how this shows up for me in my life.

I have always enjoyed being the center of attention. I know, imagine that! The baby and only son out of four kids. I can't imagine where it came from. Now, the pleasure that being the center of attention

[4] Schultz, Wolfram. "Neuronal Reward and Decision Signals: From Theories to Data." June 24, 2015. *Physiological Reviews*. https://www.ncbi.nlm.nih.gov/pmc/articles/PMC4491543/.

[5] Schultz, 2015

is something I crave, and I will leave no stone unturned looking to be at the center. One of the ways I do this is to have a few cocktails to fuel my charming character. Then, perhaps, I may slip a little too far to the left, drinking to the point where I know that the next day will be one of survival and hydration, plus a total loss of one entire weekend day. I may even do things, or at the very least say things, that I wouldn't have done or said otherwise. I may get nasty and insult a friend or, you know, push the button we know someone has that will cause a world of wounds in the relationship. Now, later on, I will clean it all up with an apology, saying, "It was just the drinks. I am really sorry," with the knowledge that everyone can relate to this and that will make it all better—*but only until the next time*!

Now, there are several ways you can weave this exercise. You could use a physical substance or whatever else it is that you find yourself saying or doing repetitively in your life that has an impact for you.

Complete Inquiry 2, then return to continue.

Whatever you got from this specific inquiry, I challenge you to look again to see if there is one that has a little more depth to it. Maybe it is something you've never admitted that, even now, if you really took that area on, will alter your life. Take a few minutes to do this inquiry again. Then, move forward to the next page. For each inquiry, you will get the maximum benefit by interacting with each question in this way.

Early Rewards

So, where did reward systems begin? Where were they fortified in our culture? I remember starting kindergarten, walking in the very first day of class and being overly excited to be away from home for the first time. I remember the moments in class—one teacher at the front of the room and one teacher in the back. Whenever we were rowdy, as five- and six-year-olds can be, one of the teachers would walk around the room with a sharpie and place little dots at the base of the palms of students who were well-behaved. At the end of the day, the person with the most dots who was, in turn, the person who sat still and behaved, earned the opportunity to choose a coveted treasure out of a little toy treasure chest. She walked around with this magic wand at the end of the day, like Glinda the Good Witch, and whomever she tapped on the shoulder or tapped on the head with this magic wand would get to pull the treasure from the chest.

You can imagine, while there was no monetary gain in the situation, there was a very priceless piece of reward. It was my first experience with pleasure and, oh how delightful and delicious it was! I got the reward. Competition was being woven into every fiber of my being and, little did I know, that would stay with me for life. It seemed so harmless through the eyes of a five-year-old. At the same time, a competitive nature was created, a pleasure system was being wired in my brain such that it would never be removed. I reveled in the acknowledgment that it was wonderful. It was the best thing that I could have experienced at that time.

Complete Inquiry 3, then return to continue.

In doing the work of considering that there have been addictions in your life, whether substances, patterns of behavior, specific actions, or roads upon which you travel, you'll notice that there are moments where all the voices inside the head begin to get a little quieter. Quieter to the point where there is absolute silence (for the first time, for many, as human beings). Continuing to interrupt these patterns of addictive, repetitive, and persistent ways you have held onto like a child with a blanket, you now can create space to connect with your soul, taking a bold action that had never been possible.

Physiologically, it makes sense, considering the ways neurons sprout and can be marked for destruction. It is also noteworthy that there's been an experience for most of mourning and depression after doing the work. These feelings that arise after doing this work I would have called depression or mourning in the past, however these don't capture the experience of life in this moment now. However, "Ascension of Being" does.

It's an absence from the body. Eckhart Tolle described it as being present. My best analogy for ascension of being can be seen in one of my favorite visualizations, in which I imagine I am sitting on the Hubble telescope and looking at the earth from a distance in the totality of darkness, yet in the presence of the light inside.

Recently, while driving home from the gym, I suddenly noticed the silence in my mind. All the voices were slowly beginning to stop. Not like the voice you hear from the outside, but the one you hear from the inside. "What what are you talking about?" That's the voice I'm talking about.

No, you aren't crazy. Just recently, I caught my mother talking to herself out loud. She said, "As long as I don't answer myself, I am fine." I encourage you to begin to answer yourself and take a bold stand against that voice inside your head that have justified your addictive behaviors for years. "It's my morals." "It's the lessons I have learned in life." "It's God guiding me." Any of these may be true and may have shaped the content of what the voice says. However, what if, just for a moment, you could create your own path? For some of you reading this, what you may have just felt is addiction, and the action that you take, which is new for you, would be the interruption I am referring to. Notice how it feels to take the new action, or notice the stagnation of continuing to allow the background phrases to control you.

Here is a little analogy that will keep getting woven through our conversation with each other. What you feel now is precisely how the addict on the street feels every time there is an opportunity to use. At this point, the sole intention of this analogy is to allow compassion to arise in your heart and soul for the ones you judge, the ones you watch on daytime television talk shows and think, without hesitation, "How awful it is for that family to allow that to happen to someone they love. Why don't they do something?"

Complete Inquiry 4, then return to continue.

Getting a Deal or Getting Taken

Now, notice that over time, you've become addicted to the concept of getting a deal. In fact, you're either addicted to "getting a deal," or you're addicted to the concept of "getting taken." Getting taken for what? Can you take for granted feeling as though you're not appreciated, valued, or respected? You're addicted to the concept of getting a deal. Look at how excited you get when you notice that there is a sale occurring at your favorite local store. While shopping, I find myself addicted to the deal. I enjoy a specific brand of juice called Suja. This particular juice happened to be on sale: buy one, get one free. In that moment, how addicted to the deal was I? I immediately took up eight bottles of the juice, knowing that I was essentially buying one getting and one free, saving half of the original cost of this juice.

So, let's look at the impact of the experience of life through the filter of getting a deal or getting taken. The impact of looking to always get a deal always results in a life of missed opportunities, due to weighing out personal worth of whatever it is you're in pursuit of against the cost in reality. When we examine the impact of getting "taken for granted" or "getting taken advantage of" or the overall experience of "getting taken," how is it affecting your life right now?

Complete Inquiry 5, then return to continue.

Can you see for yourself the constraining nature of this view of life? Notice that there is no other relationship between yourself and others. If those words don't seem to fit your situation, consider it this way: you are addicted to a world where there is "trust" and "deceit." It permeates your family, religion, relationship with God, or whatever there is for you as an outside force. It also is there, by the way, if you don't believe in God. That's just more of it. You either choose to trust or you choose not to trust. If you trust, that's similar to getting a deal. If you don't trust, that's simply you getting taken. Look at the problem from that point of view to see if there's anywhere in your life that it fits.

The Easy Way

To reveal the presence of an addiction where you may not think one exists, you simply have to look at where life is easy. We are addicted to the easier way out. Through science spaces we know molecules follow the path of least resistance. We are one big molecule that chooses the path of least resistance. But resistance to what, one may ask? The path of least resistance to the grave.

Complete Inquiry 6, then return to continue.

Being addicted to the easy way out costs you the opportunity to evolve. Begin to see how lazy we have gotten in our evolution. We are making it easier and easier to exist. For example, again we look at the current handheld computers that now serve dual purposes as telephones. The easy way out from an uncomfortable situation, such as the conversation with your family, friends, or coworkers and so many other situations, is to take yourself to the World Wide Web to look for a distraction. Or, maybe it's to get on social media, where it is far easier to communicate with others in written format versus a verbal conversation. Or perhaps you prefer to send text messages over other forms of communication.

Have you ever noticed how different people can be on social media, text messages, online dating websites, and other digital venues? Isn't it fascinating—or, at the very least, intriguing—to see how very different their persona can really be? At times, it's quite a striking difference. It's almost as if you ask yourself, "Is this the same person?" What blocks that person from communicating as they otherwise would through face-to-face communication is fear. It is fear of being with another human being. Yet again, we say that addiction to "the easy way out" has won over in these situations as well.

It truly is time for us to evolve as a species and give up the easy way out. But let's take a look at what this will really cost us. It will require a radical change in our lifestyle. Perhaps we need to give up written electronic communication. Perhaps social media was a mistake. After all, we have many samples from our past where seemingly perfect ideas ended up leading to the demise of our own health and well-being. Tobacco, alcohol, and gun control. Shall I go on?

Complete Inquiry 7, then return to continue.

Acceptance and Approval

If you haven't been able to find yourself in any other part of this journey, it is unlikely that you will walk away from this part without finding pieces of yourself. This one particular piece of addiction is the silent killer for many. Take a look for a moment at all the things you do daily for the acceptance and/or approval of others, yourself, God, or a higher power.

I will share my own personal journey with acceptance and approval. I have hesitations about letting you know that I, as your author, am a gay male. I worry that it will get in the way of the value that this book can bring to you and your life if you have a strongly held position about gay men in society based on your particular religion and spirituality. In some cultures, I would be put to death, as this is the norm in those societies. My desire is that this book penetrates those parts of the world and destroys those addictive systems that have given rise to such laws, which block one of the many expressions of humanity through sexual preference.

The deeper layer of my addiction for approval is with my family. My mother was the daughter of a Methodist minister. My sisters are all perfectly "normal" according to our society and the primitive religious morals that were all I knew growing up in the South, inside the "Bible Belt." Although outward appearances would have led most to believe I was the favorite, for decades of my life, I sought their acceptance and would do whatever it took to gain it.

I tried many methods, like introducing them to men I was dating, bringing them to the suburbs of Fort Lauderdale and exposing them to communities where gay, lesbian, and the like could be seen expressing affection openly, all to show them that I was accepted here, why not by my family? It all seemed rational to me.

All this went on for years, until a moment one evening, when I saw for myself that the very thing I was demanding and investing so much emotional energy in was the very grace that I had not allowed for my family—acceptance of how they were, without the need to change anything about themselves. It was only in that moment that acceptance fell away and suddenly my addictive need for their approval melted away. This was true empowerment.

Acceptance is a multidirectional flow of energy, and as such, it can become a trap, an addiction, if we only seek it from others rather than simply *accept* that they either will or will not. The path to true acceptance, freedom, and liberation associated with this process is understanding that we may *never* get the full respect of others that we desire or deserve, but that does not mean we cannot fully accept ourselves and fully accept the limitations of others to *accept* the totality of who we are.

The reward of approval and acceptance is one of the most abstract rewards. With many other rewards, you receive some degree of monetary gain. What I mean by abstract is that there is nothing tangible that you can touch, feel, smell, or taste. As an elementary example, when you are rewarded with candy, there is a substance to be received.

With this one, you get nothing more than a feeling, which is nothing more than a series of neurons firing in the brain, by the way. This one is the foundation of many training and development programs. They all operate on the approval of some leader or a knowing that the tenets they embody, which you are now living, are being lived out in your life and producing the results promised. I would apologize for this simplification and disruption of your world for those who are devout practitioners of the training and development programs *du jour*. However, as a former leader of training and development programs, this one is absolutely inescapable. We will discuss ongoing development in later sections. For now, let's explore various vignettes of acceptance and approval, in case you are not yet convinced.

Growing up as a teen, you placed a stake in the ground, declaring, "This is who I am." It likely was either the exact opposite of what your parents wanted for you, or it was something close to what they wanted for you. Either way, whether you followed the suggested course into adulthood or took a different path altogether, you made it your life's mission to get the approval of your parents. A word for those without parents: look in your life and see who fulfilled that role for you. Was it your adopted parents, foster parents, a grandparent or relative, a gang leader, or a friend you looked up to? There is someone there, and it's your task to identify them for the purposes of this section. Then, whatever doesn't work out, you will blame on the absence of love from your mother and/or the absence of love from your father. Or you will choose similar patterns of behavior to compensate for whatever was lacking in you or in them. This one is kind of deep, so it's okay if you have to go back and reread this one and take a pause. Keep reading on until the inquiry arises later, or maybe the next paragraph will resonate with you a little more.

Self-approval drives a multibillion-dollar industry in the world today, in the forms of fitness and cosmetic surgery. We look in the mirror, and we have that one thing that we want to change about ourselves. I have a little experience with this one as a board-certified dermatologist and cosmetic surgeon. Many people come to me with legitimate concerns for their appearance, whether it is fine lines, dark spots that they would like removed, or volume loss in the face.

They wish for these perfect imperfections to be lessened. There are patients who are in the office for the first time, those who are on their way to becoming addicted to beauty, and those who are clearly far gone. These are the patients who are constantly looking for some reason to come in or for the next procedure to do.

The fitness industry is simply another attempt at self-approval. We use health as a pretense, either for us or to please the other person in our life who matters to us. That person's point of view seems to carry a lot of weight. It provides something for you called "self-confidence." I am certainly not saying that this is good or bad. However, experience how exhausting it has become and the impact it has on those around you. I will often remind you that life doesn't happen in a vacuum, as the choices you make for yourself do not necessarily impact only you. This may be news to you, but spending two hours in the gym at night takes time away from your spouse. "I work out with my spouse/partner." Fine. Have it your way and die with amazingly fit bodies and no contribution to others, and absolutely minimal time truly being with each other. What do I mean by being with each other? It's that kind of shared human experience I mentioned earlier, for example, when you look into an infant's eyes. A few enlightened readers may know the experience I am referencing to. No, it doesn't count if you look deeply into their eyes just before sex. That's for secondary gain, if you can be honest with yourself for a moment.

Complete Inquiry 8, and then return to continue.

Alcohol and Drugs

One of the oldest addictions we are aware of is alcoholism. It's the one that has the most emotional heat and takes the blame for the demise of family units, as was the case for my own family. At this point in the book, you have a great deal of understanding about addiction. Be very clear that this conversation is not intended to provide an excuse for failing to participate in current mandated care; it is only a point of view that may give you some freedom if you are dealing with this addiction.

Alcohol is readily available, inexpensive, and often pleasing to the palate. It has extraordinary effects on the brain, creating an experience of ease in many situations and an escape from whatever it is that you are dealing with in the moment you choose to drink it. To simply call yourself an alcoholic and an addict is easy, allowing you to indulge in all the benefits thereof, like counseling, actually having a diagnosis, being a patient, and maybe even getting some time off from reality inside a treatment program to deal with life. All of this is okay. It has worked really well and altered millions of lives since the inception of this approach to alcoholism.

Illicit drugs are not as readily available as alcohol, insofar as they are not available for legal purchase. The use of these particular substances requires "drug seeking behaviors" to obtain. Similar to other reward mechanisms in life, these actions are critical to fulfillment of the addiction and have been the target of programs such as the "War on Drugs" and more recent attempts to impose the death penalty for individuals who illegally sell drugs.

What goes unnoticed is the pervasive addiction to the escape that underlies all of substance abuse. The drug or alcohol is used to escape a mind-constructed constraint for a period of time. Then, one finds oneself back within that constraint at the end of the binge or high. The operative words are "mind-constructed," given that there is nothing physical happening to an individual at the time they choose to use. Specifically, there is no impending harm or danger to one's life if they do not use or drink. (Note: this does not apply to individuals suffering from withdrawal symptoms. In this case, it is critical to life that the substance be administered.) That brief moment of the pull toward the addictive escape, similar to iron pellets in a magnetic field, is the golden opportunity to interrupt addiction to substances and many others. We will discuss more on this later.

Complete Inquiry 9, then return to continue.

Taking what you discovered about yourself in that moment, there could be some evolution occurring. Perhaps you are not a drug addict or an alcoholic. Perhaps you are an "escape addict." Even more beautiful is the who that really makes you. You are someone committed to being free in life. As someone addicted to escape and freedom, you can do so many other things to get the same experience of freedom and escape, without the deleterious health effects of using drugs or drinking.

Complete Inquiry 10, then return to continue.

Sex, Cheating, and Lying

Sex, sex, sex. While a few of you may have a good handle on this topic, many people do not have a healthy relationship with sex. What does a healthy relationship with sex mean? It is very simple—you enjoy sex without guilt or manipulation in the equation whatsoever. "Simplistic," many of you may exclaim. Take a moment and really think about this. How many of you can actually say, without a moment's consideration, that you actually meet these simple criteria?

Let's go deeper. *You relate to sex the same way you relate to money. I repeat, you relate to sex the same way you relate to money.* There's never enough of it, and you'll take it whenever you can get it, and furthermore, for some of you, wherever you can get it. Take a look at the online pornography industry if you don't believe that it's an addiction. We are including pornography in this conversation of addiction, as watching pornography and masturbating at the same time fires the same neurons that get stimulated when you actually have sex, resulting in ejaculation and orgasm. For the significant others reading, by virtue of this point of view, you are correct: your spouse is cheating on you by doing so.

Can you see that maybe this fits, just a little bit, for you in this conversation? Many of you use sex as leverage in relationships to get what you want done in the relationship. As an observer of human behavior, I see it all the time in relationships. The conversation will arise, especially between two of my dear friends. The one friend is absolutely in the role of the addict, and the partner is the one who knows, for sure, that he has the upper hand, as he only puts out a certain amount per week, just enough to get done what needs to be done around the house. Now, this fascinates me from the outside looking in. How miserable would it be to reframe something designed to be playful, fun, and rewarding to humanity in this way? Can you imagine dolphins having this issue? I think not. It is only the human, with higher-order thought, taking the action of placing value and meaning on a natural act, that can manipulate and deteriorate sex into this context.

You will take actions to seek money/sex and, if unmonitored, you will take as much of it as you can. You will *cheat* to get them if you are forced to do without them, or you will get emotional and resentful. For some of you, the cheating is what's so appealing. In fact, you may actually have sex and cheat your partner for the pleasure of taking you to climax to withhold and dominate them. This may be news for many of you, as I would bet your original thought in the conversation was that cheating was only seeking sex outside of a relationship.

Cheating may not pertain to sex. It may actually be cheating in games, on your taxes, on reporting statistics, or on your words and promises. What do I mean by this? Cheating on your words and promises is also known as lying. "I can be addicted to lying?" Absolutely. It may sound absurd to some of you, while others may be engaging in that experience right now. Truth is so confronting for many people that they avoid it at all costs. Trust is also something that is very difficult for those who lie. The assumption is that the world is as dishonest as they are.

Complete Inquiries 11 and 12, and return to continue.

Beliefs: Religion, Spirituality, Agnosticism, and Atheism

At first glance, perhaps you are wondering why I would compile such seemingly vastly opposing points of view together, and that's understandable. Underlying each of these is a belief system. Humans are addicted to our beliefs. With each of these, there is a particularly strongly held belief that there is either a god, an outside energetic force, or a resurrected deity in some capacity. Notice all the thoughts, upsetting perhaps, that arise in such a broad generalization, which may occur as a threat to religion. The need to defend and protect cannot arise unless an underlying addiction exists. Let it be for now, and let's explore this together.

Having been raised in a Methodist church by a minister's daughter, I have a bit of expertise with this one. For my family, the Christian faith was as much a part of life as the air I breathe. It was simply the way life was designed to be lived, with no deviation from this principle. Sundays, we donned our best clothes and went to church to pay reverence to Jesus Christ. This was every Sunday, and any deviation from this principle resulted in punishment, so it was always best to conform.

This area of life has always been of interest to me, as is the case with many theologists and the like. However, it arose very early on. I vividly remember the day, as a three- or four-year-old; I had not yet begun school. I asked my mother very simply, "Where did God come from?" I remember the look on her face as a young and attractive lady. She replied, "Some things we don't question, son." For me, it was a legitimate question and the kind of thing I thought about as a toddler. Is there a great designer to human beings and the experience of life? While I could delve into this topic with many citations and write a hundred pages, let's simply wonder for a moment on this topic.

As with any addiction, with this one as well, there is an escape from reality that occurs at the time of use. At the very least, practitioners experience a transcendence from reality, liberating them from current constraints. It could be the promise of an afterlife of luxury or rivers of milk and honey.

Agnostics and atheists represent a subset of addicts worth visiting. I remind you that I am a participant in this conversation as much as you are as a reader, and by no means is any of this held out to be the only truth. For the agnostic, the underlying addiction could be escaping accountability, as could be said for the atheist, where there is an absolute escape from guilt, as there is no set of spiritual laws that are honored or to which one is held accountable.

There are several other religions, but I assure you that when you substitute the same practices in Hindu, Muslim, Buddhist, or Catholic, the underlying belief provides an escape or transcendence of reality. This creates the reward of knowing that there is one simple thing called "hope." Perhaps hope for a tomorrow better than today. Hope is such a small word that provides so much relief for so many conditions, both physical and mental. It's not the word itself, however; it is the underlying given state of being.

You are addicted to hope—hope that there is an afterlife or that there isn't an afterlife or that there is a better future, including any future incarnations or afterlives. All hope gives you is an opportunity to be "hopeful" for the very best, which in the end is nothing. So, is it really the hope that gives you freedom—or is it the nothingness that arises when you are hopeful?

Complete Inquiry 13, and return to continue.

Money, Success, and Power

Welcome to the hamster wheel you will never get off of as a human. The symptoms of this addiction are excessive fatigue associated with feelings of unfulfillment and dissatisfaction with a side of always wanting more. There will never be enough. You will always have an experience of scarcity, and the realization of this is the beginning of liberation.

Look at your life as a child and the dreams you had. Personally, I knew that the level of scarcity I experienced as a child was not what I wanted for my whole life, and it fostered a drive and ambition that fueled the career I have today. Am I there yet? No, I am still trying to get to a place that matches the level of success I envision with that which I have.

For the purposes of this discussion, you could interchange the terms money, success, and power. Just think about that for a moment and see if it is a fit for you right now. You may discover that these terms carry the same feeling. The more you have, the better off you are, and you will do what it takes to get more of each.

For some people, there is a level of contentedness and a healthy relationship to each of these that will allow balance and fulfillment to be experienced. Then there are those individuals who spend their lives chasing the carrot. They rise to the next level, only to experience the same dissatisfaction, which becomes the fuel to get more. It is no wonder that we are so exhausted at the end of our day, and for some of us, at the end of our lives.

Complete Inquiry 14, and return to continue.

Suffering

Addiction to suffering is something that really has a grip to it. This one is evasive and shows up in many ways. When we hear the word "suffering," immediately what comes to mind is probably something more along the lines of torture, which is distinct. Suffering, in this case, is any action you take (or don't take) that would result in an experience of emotional pain, lack, or loss.

The abused spouse or partner that stays in the relationship for decades or a lifetime is a prime example of this. It's easy to look as the observer at someone who has risen above this state of addiction and ask, "Why don't they just leave?" It is something that is incomprehensible to imagine. However, the fact is that these people are addicted to suffering. This "abusive relationship" can take many forms, including pathologic friendships you maintain, knowing those individuals do not lift you to your higher state of being, leaving you empowered to fulfill your purpose and dreams.

Let's look a little deeper at the addiction to suffering, which is perhaps not so obvious. Many of you inflict suffering upon yourself. Others call this self-sabotage. It is what keeps you from advancing in your career, meeting your goals for physical appearance, or having the relationship of your dreams. As a mentor once told me, "If you had a crystal ball and you looked into it, would you see that you knew that this outcome would happen?" From now on, you have this book as your crystal ball, and you can see how the future will go.

You may say to yourself as well, "But that's not addiction, because there is no pleasure." While the pleasure may not be so obvious to you, it is glaringly clear to me. Sewn into this particular addiction is the addiction to comfort. For many, it is pleasurable to be allowed to continue to live a self-destructive life of suffering, rather than evolving into existence as someone who never suffers. If you have ever been told to "get out of your own way!" this may apply to you.

Complete Inquiry 15, and return to continue.

Roles

Roles in life are one of the most limiting forms of existence one could take. Some of this will seem like common sense, and at the same time we will look deeper as we go into this discussion. We will start with the first role you played in life—the child.

For most children in society who had parents or caregivers, this time of life was exquisite. It was full of playtime, free food, free shelter, and no taxes. You grew up a little, maybe got a job and a relationship, and you assumed the role of adult, with all of its responsibilities. At some point, you decided to either have children and be a parent or stay single and be a player. These divergent paths would lock your fate and direct the entirety of your life thereafter. Some of you may have gotten divorced and re-enlisted as single people, enjoying the benefits (and heartaches) thereof.

Your career or job choice is another role that you take on. For many of us, this becomes our life's sentence. It is almost like an inescapable straitjacket that we wear our entire life, experiencing only fleeting moments of freedom. You cannot *not* be inside your role that you have chosen in life and that role works beautifully for your career. However, that particular way of being so effective at making you successful at work may not be helpful in other areas of life, like your love life. Roles are not something you have. They are *something you become*. That is, they are inseparable and inescapable. One could call them "an addiction in life."

As a physician, I have an addiction to nurturing others. This addiction is so strong that it is difficult, next to impossible, to be nurtured. Let me share with you something very personal that I recently dealt with to illustrate this point.

While recently hospitalized, I found myself, yet again, confronted with an unconcealed addiction that was an honest-to-goodness celebration to discover! I have an absolute addiction to the role I play in life, called, "physician." The role of physician also includes a degree of control and integrity. We are trained in medical school, to some degree, to be "superhuman" and embrace the uniqueness that it is to be imbued with the responsibility of providing healing for humanity. We are taught to detach ourselves emotionally from a given situation and access files in the brain full of protocols for caring for disease, all while assimilating symptoms and complaints along with signs of disease, resulting in a diagnosis and management plan that provides relief of suffering and restores health. Now, if that seemed a bit much for you, that's only a fraction of what happens in split seconds, on a daily basis, in the mind of a well-trained physician.

Back to the admission to the hospital. While working one day, I had a sudden onset of intense pain upon urination, as well as chills and decreasing energy. By the end of the day, I was out the door and driving home with the heat on and the seat heaters on high on a sunny South Florida day. I knew in my heart that something wasn't right. I arrived at my home and looked in the mirror. I noticed that my skin was bright red, and I could feel radiant heat coming from my face. I concluded that, at the very least, I had a urinary tract infection. I was dehydrated and, from the color of my skin, it was likely a gram-negative bacteria that was growing in my bladder and seeping into my bloodstream, resulting in bright red skin. I bolted out the door and headed to the urgent care center down the street.

Arriving at the urgent care center, I removed myself from the role of physician. It took everything I had not overtake the situation and to allow the physician on staff do his duty and render the diagnosis and treatment plan. As I sat across the room in the room awaiting the physician to enter, I could not believe that the man across me was a physician at all. Looking at the name on his coat, I saw letters following his name consistent with him being a physician, but where was the sacred ritual of examining a patient? Where was the touch of another human being? Instead, it was surmised that this had to be a sexually transmitted disease, and I was treated accordingly.

I walked out. Why? The role of patient didn't serve me well and; in fact, it allowed my disease to progress. I felt worse than I had the day before. I took a risk and allowed another human being the privilege of controlling something as sacred as my health, and the result was worse than the beginning.

Complete Inquiry 16, and return to continue.

In short, there will be times when it may be critical to lay down your roles, allowing other parts of your life to flourish instead of being shut down and unworkable. As human addicts, your addictive nature has served you well in some areas. At the very least, if you are reading this book, none of your addictions have taken your life.

Gambling, Gaming, and Apps

Well, here we are at what I believe to be the "Mother of All Addictions," which encompasses social media and the billions of dollars we have spent on this dehumanizing attempt at connecting humanity.

Facebook, Twitter, Instagram, Snapchat, Tinder, Grindr, Match. com, and eHarmony. The ancestors thereto, including Myspace, AOL.com, and what was in the 1990s, the beginning of it all, the digital bulletin board system, where all you saw was a blinking dos cursor until someone said hello to you. While writing this particular section, ironically, on the screen as I flipped over to fulfill my addiction to social media and checked Facebook, this is what I read:

> Definitely have been questioning the daily benefit of Facebook. Wondering if freeing myself from the social media shackles would be beneficial. Each day, I read ridiculous posts from people I respect … and can't believe the amount of vitriol that is spewed. Funny thing … I'm a centrist … but the ignorance of nasty, childish, partisan bullshit has elevated my desire to eliminate this truly unhealthy addiction to the trash bin. I've always attempted to share funny things with no reference to discrimination towards anyone's beliefs. I give up. Not going to miss the very antithesis of community. You know who you are.

> Keep your personal vendettas going … and you'll
> have no one left to listen to your words! It's truly sad
> and exhausting! Bye-bye Facebook. I'm out!
> —Facebook user, published with permission

My accolades to this person, who evolved in an instant. It's a very
new concept, the "addiction" to social media, devices, and the like.
It has been so refreshing to see many begin to stand up against the
most destructive tool. To this day, I am convinced that the developers
and owners were aware of the extraordinarily addictive nature of
variable reinforcement, described in psychiatry. Specifically, what
this rule says is that if you check your phone and every time there
are alerts, you will tire of the action of checking your phone. On the
contrary, if you pick up your phone and open an app and sometimes
there are alerts while other times there are not, then this interval is
not set and predictable, and the addictive behavioral nature of the
human response is strengthened. I will take the liberty to drive this
point home.

In 2008, Jaclyn Cabral expanded on this same topic in her own way:

> Some behavioral consequences of the new digital
> brain are hyperactivity, inattention, depression,
> and multitasking mania. Based upon research for
> brain development, there is a conclusion stating that
> daily exposure to high technology stimulates brain
> alternation and neurotransmitter release; ultimately
> strengthening new pathways in the brain. The
> human mind is now learning to access and process
> information more rapidly and shift attention quickly
> from one task to the next.[6]

---

[6] Jaclyn Cabral, "Is Generation Y Addicted to Social Media?" *The Elon Journal*, Spring 2011. https://www.elon.edu/u/academics/communications/journal/archive/spring-2011-issue/.

How many times in reading this book did you find yourself checking a social media platform, whether by PC or phone? If you are one of the few who didn't follow through on the desire, how many of you at the very least thought about it or considered checking your phone or another device where social media was accessible? If you are in these two groups, you may want to close the book now and go back to the beginning, because there is a very large chance you missed something of potential value to you. If this doesn't strike you, if you haven't done this already, notice the people in the airport, in restaurants, in nightclubs, classrooms, and family living rooms who are using their smartphones, likely on a social media platform. Your life is the best evidence for anything stated in this book. There are no studies needed.

Complete Inquiry 17, and return to continue.

I look back to childhood and remember a few things about technology. The first was an old Tandy T180 computer that had a DOS prompt that came up. I would type a simple three-line program that would make the screen fill with whatever sentence I wrote. That delighted and entertained me for minutes (notice minutes only, not hours). Then there was the infamous Atari that my mother bought us. I thought the heavens had opened up until I met the Apple IIe computer, with floppy disk games. This was followed by the Nintendo, and then my very own desktop computer. It was only useful as a glorified typewriter in my time as a teen, but it was still enticing, as I would imagine all the things it would do in the future. It all seemed so innocent and harmless at the time, providing little insight into the demise it would create in humanity. This addiction would last a lifetime.

If you are beginning to feel a little tightness around your neck, it is perfectly okay at this point. You are not alone, and there is one possible answer I will propose to liberate you from this addiction.

It's very simple and takes no time at all. *Turn the phone off.* Notice your thoughts and bodily sensations as you, perhaps for a moment, consider this. The sensations are no different from the drug addict or alcoholic who has not had their fix. Suddenly, the gap between you and the "addict" may be shrinking and if it's not, you may want to flip back to the chapter on addiction to "Sex, Cheating, and Lies."

The Victim and the Martyr

Let us now take a look at an all-too-common reality for many of us. Living a life as the victim or as a martyr is an addiction robs you of something greater than joy. It robs you of your very existence. What do I mean by this? Victim mentality will perpetuate itself in every form possible. It's as if you're always at the mercy of life and never responsible for your life. Things just sort of "happen" without responsibility.

The martyr, on the other hand, absolutely will always seek out opportunities to carry the burden and take the "blame." In fact, if there is no blame, a martyr will turn things around and make it sound as if there is blame or some other impact happening or present. This will allow them to feel the degree of self-pity that characterizes this way of being. Are you beginning to get the insanity of this?

This addiction is usually found in relationships where there is perpetual disagreement. Before you begin to ponder about relationships that are human-to-human, consider less obvious relationships— international relationships, as well as people's relationship with food machines, commitments and others. To elaborate, it is our relationship to these physically and not the physicality themselves, that is the addiction.

Complete Inquiry 18, then return to continue.

Admiration

When considering admiration, one has to consider the childhood dream of fame that a select few live as their reality. From the very beginning, for every child, there is a desire for admiration from a parent, guardian, or whomever fills the role as "parent." Admiration feeds the ego very well, and therein for many begins the downward spiral.

The reward of admiration is a double-edged sword. There is, on the one hand, the drive that it gives one to excel and perhaps achieve great things. For example, being acknowledged as the top producer in a company will allow for advances not available to everyone else. The same absence of admiration suppresses others, causing resignation and cynicism, which are not unique to this particular addiction.

If the word "admiration" doesn't register for you, let's pose this a different way. How many of you find that you enjoy "winning people over"? It is that thing you do with a dash of persuasion and maybe manipulation.

Now, nobody ever died from a lack of admiration, but they could take a pretty big hit to their self-esteem. Going a bit further, the absence of that same absence of admiration, which normally fuels self-esteem, fuels depression and loneliness. Human beings have many different ways of dealing with loneliness, including healthy coping mechanisms that seek to alleviate loneliness. Unfortunately, some never escape the impact of never having admiration and ultimately turn to violent, devastating acts, such as suicide. The kicker of this "truth"—and I use "kicker" purposefully—is to watch the value you place on the admiration of your social media posts. Do you want to be admired for who you are or for the number of "likes" you receive?

Throughout this inquiry, perhaps you have thought of people whom you have impacted. I encourage you to take actions beyond your comfort zone to make a difference for others by reaching out to them and checking on them. You choose the modality—phone, text, social media messenger, or maybe even a live video call.

Complete Inquiry 19, and return to continue.

Created Rights

In the developed world, there is something called rights, for example, the Bill of Rights found in our United States Constitution. There are other types of rights. There are subtypes of rights, specific to a variety of things, including sexual preference, LGBTQ rights, women's rights, and self-created rights.

Some of those self-created rights might include the right to indulge in your various addictions. Perhaps you are addicted to being right, to validate some sense of personal value or power. However, this intense desire to be right is not something that you will give up lightly if it is an addiction for you.

Take, for instance, the current leadership in our country. President Trump is absolutely, audaciously bold about his righteousness. Any attempt at undermining his authority will result in a litany of "corrective defensive acts." There is, perhaps, a need for validation hidden inside this.

This "walking on eggshells" may show up in other relationships in your life, perhaps with your friends, family, or a coworker. The addiction to justification and explanation shows up in reality when you have to explain your point of view, feelings, positions, or behavior. Take the time to see if you can catch yourself the next time an explanation or justification begins to come out of your mouth. Notice how awkward, perhaps even impossible, it seems to maintain inner peace, or peace in the relationship, without letting the justification or explanation come to life.

Complete Inquiry 20, and return to continue.

This particular addiction can show up at any time and seems to dishonor free will like nothing else on the planet. We often feel the need to defend the rights we create. We explain and justify our actions, and we are left with the experience of never being free to choose. This is a very constraining and destructive component of this addiction. Consider that, similar to admiration, it shares the impact of diminishing self-confidence and being directly decisive, leaving behind a bit of ambivalence and hesitancy.

Complete Inquiry 21, and return to continue.

Food

While this may be obvious for many of you, it may be running in the background for others who are not yet aware of their own addiction to food. When eating for sustenance begins to deteriorate into eating for pleasure, for comfort, or to fulfill a void in one's life—eating for depression and the like—it is often seen as a phase one is going through and a part of the process whatever one is dealing with. I remember over the years of my life when there have been attempts to point the finger at additives as the scapegoat for our poor food habits. Be very clear, I am on board with you on this one.

What is it that makes food so addictive? Could it be that it is so readily available to most of the developed world? Now, of course, remove availability, and the incidence of addiction goes down, as with any other substance-based addiction. Yet this doesn't correct the underlying circuitry we have been discussing inside the human brain. Food will provide your brain with the same experience of being rewarded, and the litany of neurotransmitters, or chemicals in the brain, will impact the same areas as other drugs and addictive behaviors we have covered so far.

What's the cost of addiction? It's estimated at $107 billion per year.[7] That is an extraordinary amount of money, I think we could all agree. All for simply picking up that next bite at the table or peeling open

---

[7] Addiction.com. https://www.addiction.com/4078/top-five-costly-addictions/.

that bag of snacks and going at it. Similar to the other addictions discussed, this one absolutely has its consequences, and it's a tough one to hide. Whether it's an obese person or the frail-framed bulimic who binges and purges, you can't hide this one. If neither of these descriptions fit, then perhaps you are in a yo-yo relationship with this addiction and turn to it only in stressful times, resulting in periodic weight gain.

Again, the reference point for each of you is to be aware of the addiction to food and begin to experience compassion for those around you who may have their own concealed addiction. The response while reading about this may have been, "Thank God that's not me" or "They really have problems, amazing." That's just more of the addiction in you speaking, as you judge or compare what you are dealing with to the world around you.

My own personal journey with food has been one of addiction, evolving over the course of the ages thirty-three to forty-three. I can put a timeframe on it personally by the decline in my personal appearance weighted against what I looked like at age twenty-five. Notice the insanity inside this statement, which we will delve into more as we explore beauty addicts. Nonetheless, left to my own devices, I will eat from the time I wake up until the time I go to bed. Just before my forty-fourth birthday, I chose to deal with this addiction head-on by asking a dear friend who has a coaching empire to get me into the best shape of my life to prepare for my forty-fourth. That could not have been a more backhanded way of saying directly to her, "Help me. I can't stop eating, and I am killing myself with food."

For me, it was not until interrupting the consumption of carbohydrates that I knew how strong this addiction really was for me. Initially, I thought to myself that it was pretty easy, and then the moments came when I really couldn't do it. I broke down and had the sweet cakes (cupcakes preferred, please). As with all other addictions, there was guilt after using, the promised to cut down, and then the stark realization that breakfast was nothing more than an eye-opener.

Rising above the addiction to food has been the most empowering thing I have ever done, and I encourage each of you, with this one, to allow yourself the grace to experience life just the way it is and then be bold and release this one. You will have a transformation in your physical body and mind.

Complete Inquiries 22 and 23, then return to continue.

Complaining

As human beings, this one likely just captured many of you who had been going through the motions of reading this book to please your mentor, coach, counselor, or sponsor. If we started a twelve-step program for this little beauty, we wouldn't have enough space in a football field–sized warehouse. You are always slightly dissatisfied at some point in your life, and you will inevitably complain about something. We've dressed this one up by creating things like "suggestion boxes" and star reviews to allow us to be nice about it.

Complaining accomplishes nothing in the ears of the person listening to it. It yields nothing of good value. Yet we will do it for minutes on end. Notice the uniqueness of this particular addiction, how it arises with absolutely no effort, seeking out situations to stimulate the complaint. While some of you may subconsciously put yourself in situations that evoke complaints, for others, it just happens, no matter where they are or who they are with.

Dysphoria is the prevailing experience of the moment that gives rise to the complaint that must be vocalized. This may arise because of the service at a restaurant, a meal (for the foodies out there), the tidiness of the gym or a hotel room, or the speed limit in an area. Just pick something, and I am sure you will discover you can't imagine your life without complaining.

Complaining only arises if there is an underlying commitment, which is often unexpressed. What do I mean by this? If you complain that the service in a restaurant is not good or the care you received in a hospital is not good, you are expressing dissatisfaction that and underlying commitment, perhaps to excellence, has not been met.

Complete Inquiry 24, then return to continue.

The complaint to the recipient might be softened if you reminded them of the commitment. In expressing my complaint about the cleanliness of a hotel experience, I might say, "Good afternoon. I expect a real commitment as a guest that I and future guests will have a clean, enjoyable room. Yet, on my arrival, I noticed that the shower was broken and the floors were dirty." Can you see how the experience of the complaint is totally different? Now, imagine if in your relationship with others, with whom you surely complain, you actually expressed the background commitment with the complaint to follow. You might begin to see that anger, disagreements, separations, and divorces would disappear.

Prediction and the Past

One of the biggest rewards a person has is the incredible ability to say, "I told you so!" It is often said quite emphatically in arguments between spouses and couples, shouted at sports venues, or whatever the case may be. Another flavor of it may be when we hear the juicy words, "You were right. I was wrong." How is this addiction?

The above scenarios represent the addiction we have to predicting outcomes. In fact, while writing this book, I worked very closely with my editor. We went back and forth inside a Google doc, and he provided edits for me, which I absolutely enjoyed seeing come through. I found myself reading a few of his references one evening, and it occurred to me that his addiction was in full play.

While reading this, you may have been thinking to yourself, "Oh, yes, this sounds like another book I've read." Or perhaps you thought to yourself, as he did, "This sounds a lot like the General Systems Theory." Simply notice how you cannot allow yourself to just be in an inquiry without having knowledge of where it is going or how it is going to end up. Your whole life becomes organized around this concept of "knowing the way it goes." Then, occasionally, you will be taken out of your element, when the experience of "surprise" arises in your life's course. Did you ever wonder why the experience of being surprised is so refreshingly enlivening? It could be that, for once, you are having an experience your brain simply didn't see coming. There are other times that this happens, such as an accident.

The only difference then is your interpretation of the circumstances surrounding what happened to you. If it's pleasing, it's a surprise. If it's not, it's called disappointment or some variation thereof.

Now, how did it sit with you when I confronted you about setting out to predict your life and everything that happens? Did you find that you were a little upset, or were you discovering and addiction to your positions and points of view screaming more loudly? Your point of view and strongly held beliefs are designed so that you get to ensure the actions you take in your world are predictable.

Complete Inquiry 25, then return to continue.

Prediction is not necessarily a bad addiction to have. Certainly, when you encounter situations where you see danger or can prevent an accident, prediction is suddenly your best friend and can save your life. At the very least, it can prevent harm. So, in case you were being really heavy on yourself over this one, there is some good that can come out of some of our addictions, and this is one of them.

Perhaps one of the most powerful conversations we will explore is this hidden addiction to keeping the prediction of what will happen to you in life through repeating your past. While this may not seem obvious at first, take a moment to really look at how many times you have made the same mistake, over and over. It may be evident even in your driving record. Perhaps you have a litany of parking violations or speeding tickets. How many times have you found yourself having the experience of "the more things change, the more they remain the same?"

One of the areas this absolutely shows up is in relationships. This is especially obvious for the perpetually single or serial monogamists, who find that no matter how many people they date, the next person has the same flaws, and the relationship ends just as it began. How many times do you find yourself in a relationship and the other person says, "It seems like I have known you forever." Red flags should be going up like a five-alarm fire in midtown Manhattan. It is not that you have known that person forever physically. It's that, almost immediately and without you thinking about it, this relationship has been inserted into a set of neural pathways of addiction that have one endpoint—no other is possible. That endpoint is destruction.

Perhaps you've found yourself in similar situations, and you are just baffled as to why that is. Have you ever experienced déjà vu? There are several theories on this. Could it be simply another means of addiction, creating certain situations with certain individuals in certain places that trigger the experience of the familiar?

Some time themselves repeatedly in not-so-healthy cycles: cycles of abusive relationships, cycles of failure, or relentless cycles of near-miss overdoses. Regardless of the strong negative impact or the near-deadly outcomes, you simply continue to do the same thing over and over. We eat the wrong things for us, put the wrong things in our bodies, we make choices and take actions that we know are harmful.

Complete Inquiry 26, then return to continue.

Ongoing Development

We are addicted to the idea that there has to be a "better you," a new you, a different version of you, a transformed you—in short, that there is some kind of you other than who you really are. You are never really good enough to live and experience the life you are in, fully, without "just one more thing" that can be fulfilled by another book, another course, another session with your counselors. You may be the perpetual student who is addicted to gaining knowledge, to the point that you have escaped participating in society as a contributor and will continue to collect degrees and self-satisfying rewards to the grave.

We are so captivated by this idea that there are empires of training and development programs that deteriorate the beauty of just being into doing being as opposed to being being. This was brought to my attention when visiting with a friend who had just completed a well-known training and development course. She shared how amazed she was at the leader's example that he could stay up for hours on end and seem to have full vitality. Further accolades were given because she got to where she could generate energy. He told her that sleep was not essential and the body didn't need sleep. I chuckled at the end, as she said this leader had been with for only two of the four training days. I immediately said to myself, "That's because he was sleeping during the following two days while you were all riding the adrenaline wave."

Human beings will innately express a way of being. What do I mean by way of being? Perhaps you have ways of being upset, mad, angry. You also have ways of being happy, joyful, playful, and charming. Other ways of being will be inserted in a table, so you can review them and perhaps choose a few that resonate with you. However, we really are convinced as a species that there is some way of being better at any given moment, and we must have access to it.

Complete Inquiry 27, then return to continue.

For a moment, let's explore further the brain. The brain, very much like the heart, kidneys, and lungs, is an organ. Organs have functions in the human body, like circulating the blood through the vessels, allowing us to extract oxygen from the air we breathe to support life, and pulling toxins from our blood so we don't poison ourselves and die. There are other functions of these organs; however, for now, let's just use these to create the analogy. The brain has a function as well at the level of consciousness. It makes decisions, interprets situations to determine the next appropriate action, generates emotional responses that are appropriate to a set of stimuli, and generates those ways of being that we discussed. Interesting, eh? Let's go deeper.

For many of us, we have spent decades living a life that the brain decided was going to be the life we lived. Just like a computer, the brain has been responding to data input very much like your phone or computer responds to commands. For example, if it is cold, you turn on the heat to keep your body warm. If you are hungry, you eat food to nourish your body. If you see a fire in the room, you exit the room quickly. Simple, right?

Here is where the human brain far outsmarts a computer (at least until now). From time to time, data occurs inside the brain from inputs not even occurring in the world. The brain responds to instinct, suspicions, and concerns as if they were really happening. What do I mean by this?

Take for example, the spouse who suspects that his or her partner is cheating, even though, for the purpose of this discussion, they have not. This person will take all actions to seek to prove that their partner has been cheating and destroy the relationship, even though the partner has been completely faithful.

There are many other examples we could insert here. Rather than giving you something, it will make more of a difference for you to discover how your brain has given you the life you have lived so far, by simply reacting to people, situations, places, and circumstances in life—and you had no say, it seemed.

Complete Inquiry 28, then return to continue.

Many of you may be thinking to yourself, "Well this is simply more ongoing development in this book." You are exactly right! Your addictive prediction is correct 100 percent of the time. Some of our addictions can be used to affect the quality of our lives by making them more fulfilling. After all, some addictions are not terrible, as you have seen.

Addiction to Addiction

Freedom comes after liberation, and it is the one thing that all human beings strive for their entire life. There is the financial freedom provided by retirement for some, while, for others, it is the freedom from domination by their schedule. The paradox is that living a life given by addictions is a way to avoid being truly free. Why would we avoid the process that liberates one to live a life of freedom? Fear. In the history of mankind, fear of undergoing liberation to enjoy freedom kept people imprisoned and enslaved for decades, until one human being took a stand for people being free. No evolution is needed to live a life of addiction. No transformation is needed to live a life of addiction. Addiction is the default program of our humanity, and it's only when we interrupt the addictions as described in this book that liberation, which makes freedom possible, occurs.

We all strive towards one day being free, and yet the majority never obtain it. Many of us have participated in countless programs, read countless books, taken massive actions such as diet and exercise plans, or attended rehabilitation centers, spending thousands of dollars. Many of us may have indulged in the occasional "health retreat" to attempt to permanently interrupt the cycle of addictive patterns of behavior, only to find that we are right where we were days, weeks, or months later. These programs have been useful for us, and they have failed us. Why do these programs fail?

These programs fail because they do not deal with the underlying cause of addiction by disrupting the default program in the human brain. Consider it for a moment. There are programs for drug addiction, sex addiction, gambling addiction, the list goes on and on, and yet there is no program that deals with *addiction* addiction. Yes, addiction to addiction. That is the program we need to stop the insanity of addiction in this world. Failing to deal with addiction addiction is pulling the weed without pulling the root. It is the failure of humanity to address the root, addiction addiction—that results in us slipping back into our addictive patterns of behavior.

There, of course, is the one moment when you get a glimpse of freedom, when there's a crisis or when you're faced with death. In these moments, liberation naturally occurs, and addictions fall away. In these moments, the experience is freedom. The power of this book is that every time you distinguish an addiction in your life, or identify where addiction is running the show in your life, liberation occurs. It's now your responsibility, as a human being having read this book, to generate liberation and the resulting freedom in all areas of your life that are constrained by addictions. It is your job to cherish and nurture this liberation—your entire existence is worth it.

It is possible to experience freedom in these moments because you are fulfilling your soul's purpose. Before this incarnation, your soul existed in a state of freedom and liberation that was not required. Our souls take this incarnation clearly, knowing that these addictions will limit itself. The liberation of you, your soul, and the souls of this planet, rely upon distinguishing addiction, followed by acceptance of their presence in your life. It is our calling and opportunity to evolve, to be able to master this process so that the time spent in liberation becomes more and more and more. Addictions have served you, and now it's time to release them to fulfill your soul's purpose. That purpose is liberation.

Addicted

When a caged bird is allowed to be free, there is simply the joy of flying. When an imprisoned human is set free, there is simply the joy of living. Grant yourself that degree of freedom. In causing this breakthrough for myself in writing this book, my life is unrecognizable. There is a realm that I never knew existed. My addictions rise, and they fall away like shackles that cannot hold. This is your birthright. Know the freedom you were born to live. Fly to the heights that you were destined to achieve. You will thrive, and you will know serenity in this existence.

A powerful final inquiry to complete this journey.

Complete Inquiry 29, then enjoy your liberation.

The End and Your New Beginning

Appendix I

Grace: Empowerment after Relapse

Life rarely happens in a straight line. For the majority of those living across the addiction continuum, the line is a long and winding road, filled with its share of speed bumps and potholes. As a result, it is important to embrace successes as well as disappointments and see them not through the "black and white" eyes that are often what keep all of us stuck in the addiction cycle. Instances of "backsliding," or relapse, are arguably a part of the recovery process and the journey toward balance. Returning to one's drug of choice and/or engaging in self-destructive behaviors is certainly not the ultimate goal, but we all need to walk through the fire more than once if we want the full and fulfilling lives we have committed to achieve.

Historically, relapse has been seen as a weakness of character, but what if the paradigm was seen through a different lens—one that offers the possibility that no action, reaction, or human experience is without worth, without truth, and without opportunity to gain greater insight into how to engender lasting change? Relapse is not an expression of failure; instead, it is a necessary benchmark of success and therefore part of recovery. In truth, many recovering addicts have one or more relapses: Up to 60 percent of patients who receive substance-abuse treatment will relapse within one year, [8] and the relapse rate is even higher for some drugs, like heroin. Gambling addiction has similar rates: About 50 to 75 percent of gamblers resume gambling after attempting to quit.[9]

The most important part of this journey is to understand that recovery is a reflection of the human experience, and, as perfectly imperfect humans, this commitment to self is a lifelong healing process. Do not use a relapse as yet another tool for self-flagellation. Instead, recognize it as a reminder that you need to reevaluate and modify your strategy.

Begin by embracing relapse, as it is not the enemy. You do not have to have all the answers right now. What is integral and inspiring is your desire to move past your relapse and forward with your recovery. That grace is at the forefront of who you are and why you are on this journey.

---

[8] Slomski, Anita. "Mindfulness-Based Intervention and Substance Abuse Relapse." *JAMA Network*. June 25, 2014. https://jamanetwork.com/journals/jama/article-abstract/1883017.
[9] "Feelings and Situations That Precede Gambling Relapse." National Center for Responsible Gaming. April 14, 2011. http://blog.ncrg.org/blog/2011/04/feelings-and-situations-precede-gambling-relapse.

Appendix II

1. Addiction is real.

2. Addiction is a part of life.

3. Not all addicts are face-down in a ditch.

4. Addiction protects us but also traps us.

5. We are all wearing *at least* one of the addiction masks.

6. Confronting and dealing with *addiction* addiction is a possible answer.

Appendix III

Original thoughts that sourced this book I wanted you to have. May they enliven you the way they enlivened me.

Pleasure is a source of our de-evolution and the extinction of human beings. What will prevent our further evolution is the need for immediate gratification, which nurtures pleasure. When someone takes a drug, behavior, or action consistent with addiction, pleasure is experienced. Addiction is a viral infection, replicating unnoticed. It has masterfully escaped immune surveillance for centuries. Undistinguished as a virus, it exists only as something that cannot affect us. What then is the vaccination to prevent the development of this virus in future generations? Awareness of its existence is the opportunity to incite change that will alter life.

Teas and spices were an early form of reward and currency. It generated an empire no different from the current drugs of abuse. Currency is traded on paper or metal, assigned values that we designate. It is only when our source of pleasure and fulfillment is located outside of us that we find ourselves in this vicious circle of addiction. If what fulfills me is located within me, then I need nothing from the outside world to bring me pleasure and fulfillment. To be happy, fulfilled, and content with oneself is to be fully evolved. At this point, nothing more is needed to fuel any addiction-fulfilling behaviors.

What if admiration was the original sin? Or was it desire? It is no coincidence, and what has been undistinguished is simply that the original sin involved the following patterns of behavior:

1. Pleasure—an experiential phenomenon whereby human beings escape reality/law. Man was forbidden to eat the fruit, which is underneath desire in Buddhism.
2. Choice—judgment.
3. Action—defying ourselves and reality, sort of the superhero or the villain.
4. Impact—if positive, immediately repeating the behavior and, if negative, seeking a temporary redemption (confession) or fix (anything that alleviates the suffering) until that next opportunity to escape reality and experience pleasure occurs.

The threat of being found out as an addict is as powerful a reinforcement as a reward. Admiration of the hero and villain is taught very early on in our cartoons. Good deeds are applauded. When the original laws were given to us, they completely backfired due to this network of neurons in the human brain. Examples are everywhere, from Adam and Eve to current laws in any country. What goes undistinguished, and was so beautiful, is the original beauty of unity in the garden of life. The intention could have been to nurture our fellow humans' survival. The action was vilified by the church. The story of what happened is strictly a matter of interpretation. The story made for a great division and spread like a virus with the adoption of this notion by every aspect of humanity regardless of the miles of separation. Or was the original action rooted in causing admiration and need for another?

There is the intention of the law, and there is also the intense and unrelenting pull to escape the law. Law is stated in language, designed to control or determine our actions. Now we are addicted to this concept of division. The mere notion of being one species, together, taking actions committed to the survival of each, is limited by the inability of mankind to interrupt and be greater than the experience of pleasure that arises when control of others is exerted.

The source of every moment of suffering is a law. We suffer because of laws. Laws of beauty, laws of physics, laws of the land. Sins of omission and commission. However, is it impossible for us to all adopt and redirect our actions in a single instant back toward the original design: giving to those in need. Originally, the gods saw a need. The perceived need was laws. If the laws were given by God, they would unite and not divide. This is not to say that all laws should cease, or should they? While the objectives and goals of a race have always been looking for something more in others, in our universe, in the future perhaps, the entire time our destiny and the answer to all suffering lies in our past. We are, to a degree, prisoners of law.

If we as humans could, without impending doom or further loss, commit to taking an action that served every human on this planet, our species would survive. Oneness has been collapsed into the cause of pleasure to arise in others or participating in actions that cause pleasure to arise in ourselves.

Now, notice what immediately arises: the addiction/attachment to the fulfillment of your own pleasure. If you adopt this theory, you relinquish your self-created right to pleasure on the one hand, and, on the other, you disappear. All that there is is being.

Afterword

Here you are, exactly where you began. You are physically unchanged, still breathing. Nobody got hurt, and you are as wonderful as you were when you started. Certainly, I think we can all agree that there has been at least some insight that was gleaned along the way, and then there are those of you who, like myself, absolutely can never see the world the same way after this experience together. The greatest difference between then and now is that you've been liberated from the addiction that is fueling the insanity of human beings. Living a liberated life requires you to be the kind of human being who can cause things to shift in the world, and especially for yourself, with velocity and ease. By now, you've explored the deepest parts of your life that contributed to the stagnation of your existence, and I've taken that journey with you. For some of you, this may have been just another read, and it will sit with the collection of hundreds of other titles and courses you've completed. That's fine, and there's nothing wrong with that. At the very least, you have fueled the addiction to experiencing that there is more than what this moment is.

Liberation provides you with one single position that gives an extraordinary amount of freedom and play to your life. The position simply is, "I am a human being with addictive tendencies. I am not addiction." If you're not an addict, which you're not, then who are you? That is completely an invention inside your new freedom and responsibility in completing this work.

The invitation is very simple. If this book worked for you, share it with someone in your life fearlessly and allow them the same opportunity. If the book didn't allow you to experience liberation from your addictive tendencies, then share that with someone as well. If you are at the point of thinking to yourself, "I'm just not sure this was of any use to, me but there was that one addiction he mentioned," then share that with someone else.

As you share about your experiences, you will experience the joy that it is to liberate another. Why would men like Nelson Mandela, Martin Luther King Jr, Mahatma Gandhi, or the Pope have devoted their entire lives to the liberation of another human being, other than it is worth every fiber of their being? You have a unique opportunity to dwell among the greatest of all beings of all time. Let this be your time. Humanity needs you now more than ever.

Let us rise to the purpose of liberation of this planet. Please share your experience by emailing me directly at info@AddictedTheBook.com, or keep the conversation alive and evolving by joining the online forum. For now, I have one last request. Simply take a moment and reflect on your journey. Look back through your notebook at your response in the beginning of the book when I asked you the simple question: "Why did you choose to read this book?" Write down as much as you can, and include emotions and memories that you had when you chose to buy the book, the hopes and dreams you have that you would like to see fulfilled if possible at the end of this journey.

Namaste

Workbook

Inquiry 1: Take ten minutes to make yourself a list for of the "must-haves" that are your addictions. Notice how you feel at the very thought of life without these?

_____

_____

_____

_____

_____

_____

_____

_____

_____

_____

_____

_____

_____

_____

_____

Inquiry 2: Where in your life do you find that the reward is so appealing that you will continue making choices to do or say things to get that reward, while sacrificing something you truly value?

_____

_____

_____

_____

_____

_____

_____

_____

_____

_____

_____

_____

_____

_____

_____

_____

_____

_____

_____

_____

Inquiry 3: Take a few minutes for yourself to see how, as a child, there might have been similar systems in place that you experienced. What were your early rewards? Can you see how you were just along for the ride and you had no idea what was happening?

Inquiry 4: This inquiry is a little bit more than your usual inquiry. For now, go find a mirror. Look yourself in the eyes and begin to experience the impact of years of addiction on your life. Perhaps you've discovered at least one addiction you have that you can work with. What emotions arise?

_____

_____

_____

_____

_____

_____

_____

_____

_____

_____

_____

_____

_____

_____

_____

_____

_____

_____

_____

_____

Inquiry 5: Take about ten minutes and look for areas of your life where you feel as though you're either having an experience of getting taken. What are those areas of life that you're getting taken? Now, take it a step further. When you're actually getting that deal, are you in the experience of getting taken?

Inquiry 6: How do you feel right now knowing that you have been spending your entire life addicted to the easiest way out? What has being addicted to the easy way out cost you in your life?

_____

_____

_____

_____

_____

_____

_____

_____

_____

_____

_____

_____

_____

_____

_____

_____

_____

_____

_____

Inquiry 7: Take a few moments for yourself and look to see where your addictions to the easy way out exist. What is it costing you? Is that really worth it? Can you see for yourself how there's been no evolution for your own life?

_____

_____

_____

_____

_____

_____

_____

_____

_____

_____

_____

_____

_____

_____

_____

_____

_____

_____

_____

_____

_____

Inquiry 8: Look for yourself into your world and see if you can identify where you are addicted to approval of others, self-approval, or approval of a higher power (or God). We will spend deeper time in that subject later, and if it will make you feel that you are getting something of value here, use it for now and we will go deeper into it later.

_____

_____

_____

_____

_____

_____

_____

_____

_____

_____

_____

_____

_____

_____

_____

_____

_____

_____

Inquiry 9: For now, look at your life if this section applies to you, and speculate on what you are trying to escape when you use or drink. Can you see how maybe it's not the substance you are addicted to but the escape?

_____

_____

_____

_____

_____

_____

_____

_____

_____

_____

_____

_____

_____

_____

_____

_____

_____

_____

_____

_____

_____

Inquiry 10: What are some of the things that you could now participate in that would bring about freedom and allow for an escape that you might not have been aware of?

_____

_____

_____

_____

_____

_____

_____

_____

_____

_____

_____

_____

_____

_____

_____

_____

_____

_____

_____

_____

Inquiry 11: Explore your relationship to sex. How do you use sex to achieve what you want or to manipulate your partner? What is the impact on your relationship to them and with yourself?

Inquiry 12: Explore all the little cheats and lies in your life. What has been the benefit to you, and then, what has it cost you in those areas of your life?

_____

_____

_____

_____

_____

_____

_____

_____

_____

_____

_____

_____

_____

_____

_____

_____

_____

_____

_____

_____

Inquiry 13: What has your addiction to beliefs cost you in your life, and where are you hopeful, at best, in life?

_____

_____

_____

_____

_____

_____

_____

_____

_____

_____

_____

_____

_____

_____

_____

_____

_____

_____

_____

_____

_____

_____

_____

_____

Inquiry 14: Who have you left behind because they were not powerful, admirable, or wealthy enough that could have made a difference for your life? Perhaps you were "riding the tails of their success" and a co-dependency arose. What's this been like for you?

_____

_____

_____

_____

_____

_____

_____

_____

_____

_____

_____

_____

_____

_____

_____

_____

_____

_____

Inquiry 15: List how addiction to suffering may show up in your life, and what is the immediate impact on you? How about the impact on others in your life? Hint: you may ask someone in your life how this has impacted them. How has suffering served you in your life?

_____

_____

_____

_____

_____

_____

_____

_____

_____

_____

_____

_____

_____

_____

_____

_____

_____

_____

_____

Inquiry 16: Where in your life have you laid down your addictive roles and found yourself in an uncomfortable, maybe even dangerous, situation, and then immediately went back to your more snug and comfortable addictive roles?

_____

_____

_____

_____

_____

_____

_____

_____

_____

_____

_____

_____

_____

_____

_____

_____

_____

_____

_____

Inquiry 17: Notice where social media has affected your life and relationships with the people around you. What has been the impact on those relationships and your relationship to yourself?

_____

_____

_____

_____

_____

_____

_____

_____

_____

_____

_____

_____

_____

_____

_____

_____

_____

_____

_____

_____

_____

Inquiry 18: What does the victim constantly escape in life by assuming this role? What does the martyr escape in life by assuming this role? What's the impact in your life with a lifetime of this addiction?

_____

_____

_____

_____

_____

_____

_____

_____

_____

_____

_____

_____

_____

_____

_____

_____

_____

_____

_____

Inquiry 19: How has admiration influenced the past for you? Was it an excess of admiration or absence of admiration that caused excessive "longing to belong?"

_____

_____

_____

_____

_____

_____

_____

_____

_____

_____

_____

_____

_____

_____

_____

_____

_____

_____

_____

_____

_____

Inquiry 20: What obvious self-created rights do you have that are influencing your path in life? If any of these rights are disempowering you or acting as obstacles to a full and fulfilled life, identify them, along with at least one way you can choose differently.

Inquiry 21: What are your recurring justifications that show up for you in life, and how do they limit your passion for people? Take each opportunity to notice how often you use justifications and explanations. What would your relationships be like without them?

_____

_____

_____

_____

_____

_____

_____

_____

_____

_____

_____

_____

_____

_____

_____

_____

_____

_____

_____

_____

Inquiry 22: Who could you share with in your life about your own addiction to allow them some freedom to share with you about their potential addictions?

_____

_____

_____

_____

_____

_____

_____

_____

_____

_____

_____

_____

_____

_____

_____

_____

_____

_____

_____

_____

Inquiry 23: Notice the discomfort we have when talking with others about our lives. Is there a hidden addiction constraining your ability to share with others?

Inquiry 24: Write down your recurring complaints and see if there is an underlying theme in your life that is a commitment that if expressed could change relationships.

_____

_____

_____

_____

_____

_____

_____

_____

_____

_____

_____

_____

_____

_____

_____

_____

_____

_____

_____

_____

Inquiry 25: Speculate on ways your addiction to being able to predict outcomes influences your life and shapes your reality.

Inquiry 26 from: What parts of your life in "keeping the past alive" are most affected by this addiction? Is it romance, personal health, career, relationships with your parents or relatives, or your relationship to yourself that is most influenced? Note: You may notice many areas where this addiction is affecting you. Write them all down.

_____

_____

_____

_____

_____

_____

_____

_____

_____

_____

_____

_____

_____

_____

_____

_____

_____

_____

Inquiry 27: What way of being do you resist that you wish would go away? Said another way, what are your self-perceived flaws that you believe life would be greater without?

Inquiry 28: Looking at your life now, what are some real-life instances where your relationship to others, or the actions you took with others, were at least influenced if not fully determined by the brain.

_____

_____

_____

_____

_____

_____

_____

_____

_____

_____

_____

_____

_____

_____

_____

_____

_____

_____

_____

Inquiry 29: If your life really isn't about all these addictions, what could it be about now?

About the Author

Dr. Will Richardson's background as a Molecular Cell Biologist taught him to always look at how each small part contributes to the whole of life. His passion for art and service of humanity came to life as he found his way and became a leader of Dermatology in South Florida at his practice Natura Dermatology & Cosmetics. This provided him with an opportunity to experience life fully and further develop himself by participating in training and development programs that he later went on to lead.

At the core of who he was Dr. Richardson knew that his existence was for a greater purpose beyond his reach. During a time of complete dissolution of ego he saw the beauty in his own existence and became committed to bringing it to life to share with others. Dr. Richardson sets a new precedence bridging the gap between addiction, training and development and spirituality. Addicted: From Obstacle to Opportunity is his first publication that fulfills what he saw missing in human evolution and the resultant liberation that humanity deserves.

Dr. Richardson currently resides in South Florida and enjoys reading, writing and boating during his spare time. He enjoys peaceful living and meditation in his private studio in his home.

Printed in the United States
By Bookmasters